Dictionary of Cooking Terms

For the Beginner Cook: Includes abbreviations, terms, and techniques

PAULA C. HENDERSON

ISBN-13: 978-1722896294
ISBN-10: 1722896299

CONTENTS

DICTIONARY OF COOKING TERMS

NOTES

....

....

....

....

....

....

....

....

....

....

....

....

....

....

....

....

....

....

....

....

....

....

....

....

I wish you much success!

Whether you are learning to cook for yourself, your family, or be of service to others.

Wishing You a lifetime of good health.

AN ALPHABETIC LIST OF COOKING TERMS, ABBREVIATIONS, AND TECHNIQUES

1. ACV: Apple Cider Vinegar

2. Al Dente: cooked but still firm to the bite

3. Aioli: Originally garlic, olive oil and egg whipped to form a mayo style sauce or spread.

4. Antipasto: Italian for a plate consisting of an assortment of appetizers

5. Aperitif: a drink taken prior to a meal in order to stimulate appetite.

6. Appetizer: Small portion of food eaten prior to an entrée. Sometimes referred to as hors d'oeuvres.

7. Arrowroot: a plant based starch used as a thickening agent. Used in place of traditional cornstarch. Can usually be found in most supermarkets next to the cornstarch. A good alternative for those avoiding corn and grain products.

8. Aspic: jellied meat, fish or stock. A savory jelly made with meat stock that has been 'set' in a mold.

9. Au Jus: dipping sauce made from a meats own juices that are developed while cooking. Sometimes referred to as drippings.

10. Au Lait: a French term referring to a dish being served with milk.

11. Bake: to cook in the oven on the bake setting

12. Barbecue: This depends on what part of the country you are in. Some say barbecue when referring to grilling outdoors on a grill. Others are referring to meats that have been slow cooked in a special barbecue sauce.

13. Baste: to brush or pour fat, broth or sauce onto a food while it is cooking to add flavor or keep moist.

14. Beat: to mix quickly for the purpose of mixing all ingredients into a smooth consistency.

15. Bias: To cut on an angle.

16. Bisque: a thickened, creamy soup

17. Blackened: spice coated fish or chicken seared quickly over high heat in a pre-heated cast iron skillet or grill to cause a noticeable char.

18. Blanch: to briefly boil.

19. Bind: to thicken a heated sauce or soup using a binder such as flour or eggs.

20. Braise: term used when cooking a large piece of meat, such as a roast, partially covered in liquid.

21. Boil: Bubblies have formed

22. Brine: A salty solution used for pickling, curing or tenderizing protein or vegetables.

23. Broil: using direct, close heat.

24. Broth: stock is a broth made from boiling meats with the bone-in. Broth is made by boiling meats that are boneless. A stock (bone-in) will have a deeper flavor whereas a broth (boiling meats without the bone) will give you a lighter broth.

25. Brown: to sauté' a food until visibly browned

26. Butterfly: To split a food item nearly in half (usually meat or fish). When you are butterflying an item, you do not cut all the way through, making sure to have two pieces slightly attached at one edge. An effort to create one larger, but thinner piece of meat as in a chicken breast.

27. c: cup

28. Capers: Found in the aisles of you supermarket in a jar. Capers are the small buds of a Flinders bush. They are pickled in vinegar or dried and salted.

29. Caramelize: to cook slowly on the stove top until the food has become brown and sweet

30. Chiffonade: Term used to describe knife cuts that results in thin, long pieces of herbs or greens. To make this cut, stack leaves (like basil) on top of each other, roll together, and slice thinly.

31. Chutney: a relish of fruits, spices and sometimes herbs. Usually served alongside meats.

32. Clarify: to remove impurities usually by boiling. Once the impurities have been removed either by pouring through a strainer or putting in the refrigerator and allowing to separate the food has been clarified.

33. Confit: meat cooked in its own fat.

34. Core: to remove the 'core' or inedible middle portion of a fruit like the core of an apple or pineapple

35. Cornichons: an old term that has started to trend again! A cornichon are small, whole, pickles.

36. Cream: to change a solid into a creamy consistency such as with butter or shortening. Usually by beating the solid after it has been allowed to get to room temperature.

37. Crepe: very thin and somewhat delicate pancake. Crepes can be stuffed with sweet or savory foods for breakfast, brunch, lunch or supper.

38. Crimp: a decorative term as in when working with the edges of dough

39. Crudites: Assortment of raw vegetables.

40. Cure: preserving meats by drying, salting, or smoking.

41. Cut-in: to cut in a cold food with a room temperature food by using a knife or fork so as to cut up the cold food, like butter, while blending.

42. DF: or df: Dairy Free

43. Deglaze: after removing cooked meat from a skillet the act of pouring liquid into the pan and then scraping the bottom to loosen the bits of the meat for the purpose of making a sauce.

44. Degrease: is to remove fats or oils from foods. Such as to skim the top of a soup, stew or stock (broth) or even meats that are cooking. Sometimes after a stock has been refrigerated and the grease, or fat has floated to the top.

45. Doz Dozen (12 items makes a dozen)

46. Dredge: to drag foods through egg or flour for the purpose of coating

47. Dress: to toss with a dressing.

48. Drippings: fat juices produced from cooking meat

49. Emulsify: to combine two ingredients that do not naturally combine. A good example would be lemon juice and mayo. You have to stir or whip them together.

50. Entrée: Main course.

51. EVOO: Extra virgin olive oil

52. Fillet: not to be confused with filet. A filet is a cut of boneless meat. To fillet is to remove the bone from a cut of meat.

53. Filo: paper thin pastry used as wrappers for sweet or savory foods.

54. Flambé': foods that have been doused in some form of alcohol and then lit by a flame to cause it to flame.

55. Florentine: a descriptive term used when a food is served with spinach.

56. Flute: to create decorative or fancy grooves usually on pastry or pie crusts.

57. Fold: Not the same as stirring or mixing. This is a method of blending ingredients by which you slowly and carefully go around the perimeter of the bowl, then going under the ingredients keeping your utensil in contact with the bottom of the bowl and back to the surface all in one motion. This point of this motion is to move the contents around, under and then to the surface of the bowl. A gentle blending if you will.

58. Fricassee: A meat that has been cooked by the technique of braising. To braise a meat you fry, or brown it lightly on both sides and then transfer to a slow cooking method such as in the oven.

59. Frittata: an egg based dish similar to an omelet. The difference is that you combine the vegetables, meats and cheeses with the eggs for a frittata then transfer to a skillet to be started on the stove top. Finishing off in the oven. An omelet has vegetables, meats and cheeses added after the eggs have been in the skillet and the eggs are folded over them.

60. Fritter: deep fried dough that is filled with fruit or meat, cheeses or vegetables.

61. Ganache: a whipped filling of chocolate and cream

62. Garnish: Enhancing a dishes appearance with something colorful like a lemon wedge, sprig of parsley or chopped scallions.

63. Glaze: can refer to drizzling icing over a dessert or washing a pie crust with egg white.

64. GF: sometimes gf: Gluten Free

65. GRFR: Grain Free

66. g - gram

67. Grate: like shreds. To grate a cheese or vegetable using a grater that creates small shreds of the food.

68. Gratin: when a food is topped with something that has then been browned to form a browned crust on the top. Usually breadcrumbs.

69. Grease: to coat a pan with butter or oil. "To grease the pan".

70. Horseradish: a good alternative to add heat to your dishes if you avoid nightshades. Horseradish is a root. You can find it in your produce department or in the aisles with condiments as a prepared horseradish usually in a jar. Goes well with roast beef!

71. lb: pound

72. lg large

73. Lard: A solid fat for use in cooking. Derived from a pig.

74. Julienne: a style of cutting vegetables into long thin strips.

75. Knead: to 'work' dough. By hand or by a mixer with a special attachment. By working or kneading the dough it makes the dough more elastic by developing the glutens in the flour.

76. Macerate: A technique by which you set something, usually a soft fruit like strawberries in sugar or a flavored liquid. Tossing berries in sugar to macerate them will pull the natural juices out of the berries and make a sauce.

77. Marble: gently blending two foods in such a way that you can still tell the difference in where the two foods are. Like a swirl.

78. Marinate: Sometimes referred to as "marry" when you soak meat or vegetables in a liquid to absorb flavors.

79. med medium

80. Meringue: Egg whites that have been beaten with sugar to form a stiff whipped cream like topping for desserts.

81. Meuniere: a technique of preparing foods. First you dredge the food in flour and then sauté in butter. A meuniere sauce is brown butter, chopped parsley and lemon juice. To make brown butter you simply place real, unsalted butter in a skillet and 'simmer' stirring frequently until it turns a golden brown color. This process must be watched the entire time as it will easily burn.

82. mg milligram

83. Mince: A cutting technique that leaves the food cut into smaller pieces than dicing.

84. NSFR: nightshade free

85. oz ounce

86. Pare: to remove the skin of a fruit or vegetable.

87. Parboil: partial boiling of food

88. Pinch: To grasp a small amount of something in order to sprinkle it over food; an imprecise measurement roughly equivalent to 1/16 teaspoon.

89. Pit: to remove the pit, or seed of a fruit or vegetable

90. pkg package

91. Planked: cook on a thick piece of hard wood.

92. Poach: cooking a food by partially submerging it in liquid

93. Polenta: another term for mush or grits made from cornmeal or farina.

94. Potage: soup

95. Prosciuto: paper thin slices of cured meats.

96. Pt pint

97. Puree: cooked food that has been blended to a creamy consistency

98. Qt quart

99. Reconstitute: to restore a dried food to its original state by adding liquid

100. Reduce: to cook down. The point of this is to make a more concentrated flavor or to thicken.

101. Render: to render means to cook the fat out of the food. Usually by cooking slowly.

102. Rest: Allowing a food to sit after removing from heat prior to slicing.

103. Rind: much like the skin but usually this term is reserved for the thick skin on fruit that one might zest

104. Roast: to cook on low heat for an extended period of time. Usually by dry heat in an oven.

105. Roux: flour and fat combined to be used as a thickener.

106. SF: soy free

107. Sauté: to cook quickly over high heat

108. Scald: to bring a temperature just below the boiling point.

109. Scallop: to cook with a cheese sauce

110. Score: small narrow cuts on the surface of a food

111. Sear: cooking a food on the stove top, in a skillet until a crust forms. Usually a meat.

112. Seize: when a sauce becomes hardened and lumpy

113. Set: this depends on the food you have prepared but for example if you make jello and put the watery liquid in the refrigerator. Once it turns into jello that you would eat means that it has "set".

114. Sift: to pass through a sifter, mesh strainer, or wire strainer for a finer texture.

115. Simmer: to cook at a low heat at a "just" boiling point.

116. Simple Syrup: is a mixture of equal parts of water and sugar

117. Skim: to remove fat that has risen to the surface of liquid while cooking

118. sm small

119. sq Square

120. Steam: to cook by steam alone in a double boiler.

121. Steep: to allow an ingredient like a tea bag or herb to soak in water for a period of time to flavor the water. Best when covered.

122. Sterilize: a method of destroying micro-organisms by boiling, dry heat, or by steaming.

123. Stew: to simmer on low heat for an extended amount of time.

124. Stock: stock is a broth made from boiling meats with the bone-in. Broth is made by boiling meats that are boneless.

125. t: teaspoon (a lower case 't' is meant to refer to a teaspoon as an upper case 'T' would refer to a Tablespoon.)

126. tsp: teaspoon

127. T: tablespoon (a lower case 't' is meant to refer to a teaspoon as an upper case 'T' would refer to a Tablespoon.)

128. Tenderize: to tenderize meat is to make it tender. Usually done with a kitchen tool like a mallet or by using an acid like lime juice.

129. Truss: securing poultry or fowl with strings or skewers to hold its shape while cooking.

130. Yield: yield means the same thing as number of servings.

131. Zest: to grate the skin or rind of a fruit.

CHEESE

American cheese: a processed cheese made from a blend of milk, milk fats, milk solids, and whey.

Blue cheese: Easily identified by the blue vein running through the cheese. A distinctive sharp taste and smell. Blue cheese can be hard and crumbly, or it can be melted down.

Brie: a soft cow's milk cheese. Has a mild, tangy and nutty flavor. Generally baked and eaten warm.

Camembert: a cow's milk cheese, has a somewhat sweet taste with an earthy smell.

Cheddar: there are many varieties of cheddar cheeses. From sharp to mild and good eaten cold or heated.

Cotija: A cheese of Mexico made from cow's milk. From the family of the parmesan cheeses this cheese is crumbly and dense. A strong salty flavor. Not a good choice for melting but rather to crumble over the top of your favorite Mexican dishes.

Cottage cheese: A cheese curd product where the curd is drained but not pressed. Made from cow's milk made from the milk leftover after making butter.

Cream cheese is made from cow's milk and originates from the United States. A creamy, spreadable product made from the unskimmed cow's milk combined with cream. It is made firm by using lactic acid. Cream cheese has a general mild, sweet taste with a pleasant tang.

Feta cheese is made from goat's milk or sheep's milk. Not traditionally cow's milk but you can find cow's milk feta in most supermarkets. A product from Greece with a strong nutty, salty and tangy flavor.

Goat cheese less lactose than cow's milk. It generally has a stronger flavor than cow's cheese

Gorgonzola is a variety of blue cheese made obvious by the blue vein. Gorgonzola can be quite salty

Gouda cheese is a product of the Netherlands. A semi-hard cheese that is generally crumbly, dense with a full flavored pungent sweet taste.

Gruyere cheese comes to us from Switzerland. Traditionally known as a semi-soft cheese and slightly grainy with a taste that has been described as fruity and nutty.

Havarti is a lovely creamy, semi-soft cheese with a smooth texture. This cheese has a buttery, creamy and sweet flavor.

Mascarpone originates from Italy. Made with cow's milk. This has a creamy, smooth and spreadable texture. Mascarpone is made by curdling milk cream with citric acid or acetic acid.

Monterey jack a white cheese made in Mexico and the United States. Made from cow's milk the texture is described as supple and creamy with a mild taste.

Mozzarella cheese is what most of us use on our pizza. It has a milky taste.

Parmesan cheese made from cow's milk with a sharp nutty and savory taste.

Pimento cheese: A spreadable mixture of raw cow's milk, spices and mayonnaise. Pimento Cheese originated from the United States.

Provolone is an Italian cheese made from cow's milk. A firm, grainy texture. With a mild taste.

Queso is traditionally used in Mexican dishes. An un-aged cheese with a mild, milky taste.

Ricotta cheese. From Italy. Ricotta is suitable for persons with casein intolerance.

HERBS AND SEASONINGS

- BASIL: Easy to grow at home or find in your local grocery store this herb is the most popular used to make pesto.

- BAY LEAVES: A hint of lemon flavor, use whole leaf but remove before serving. Good in soups and when simmering beans.

- CAYENNE PEPPER: Ground dried cayenne chili pepper. Cayenne pepper is a nightshade.

- CILANTRO: Green, leafy herb best purchased and used fresh from your produce department. Dried ground cilantro does not taste the same as fresh.

- CINNAMON: More and more this spice is being used for savory dishes but traditionally used in baked goods.

- CUMIN: A smoky seasoning and can be an excellent replacement for those avoiding paprika which is a nightshade.

- CURRY POWDER: Purchase this blend or make your own by mixing coriander, cumin, chili powder, and turmeric.

- DILL: A beautiful plant and easy to use. Also can be purchased in the dried seasoning section.

- GARLIC: What form you purchase may depend on how you will be preparing it. Garlic powder, minced garlic in a jar, or fresh garlic bulbs. Did you know you can freeze fresh garlic bulbs? Just place in a freezer bag as is.

- GINGER: Best when you buy a ginger root found in your produce department. Just place the root in a

- OREGANO: Aromatic spice used for Italian dishes, chicken and other meats.

- PAPRIKA: (paprika is a nightshade) Used for its smoky flavor, try cumin as a substitute if you are avoiding nightshades.

- PARSLEY: Best when enjoyed fresh and no need to limit this herb to a garnish on the plate. Toss a handful in with salads, make a pesto or salsa verde and more.

- ROSEMARY: A woody herb best used when slow cooking a roast or chicken.

- SAGE: Wonderful herb for all kinds of dishes. Try roasted sage chicken!

- THYME: Thyme can enhance almost any dish. Take a sniff to see if it might go well with what you are having for supper tonight. Good in soups, stews, on meats and vegetables.

LETTUCE AMAZE YOU!

1. Arugula: A tender lettuce with a peppery taste. Nice lettuce for a mixed green salad. Goes well with a vinaigrette.

2. Bibb: A mild tasting lettuce with a tender texture similar to spinach.

3. Endive: Mildly bitter taste. The lighter the leaves, the more mild the taste. Texture is tender but firm so a great choice for dipping.

4. Frisee: Slightly peppery taste. Tender leaves. Best served cold. Great for a mixed greens salad and for use in making a pesto.

5. Iceberg: A bright crisp mild lettuce. Refreshing and watery. Great choice for use in homemade salad dressings, dips and sauces. Great choice when making lettuce cups. Contrary to what we are told this lettuce is nutritious and very hydrating. Great for dry

skin, induces a sense of well-being when eaten on a regular basis.

6. Kale: A dark green hearty, leafy green. Taste is a bit milder than spinach. Perfectly okay to purchase fresh or frozen (without sauces or spice). Great to keep on hand as a freezer staple and then buy fresh as a recipe may call for it. Okay to eat raw or cooked but please note: if you have thyroid disease you should limit consumption to cooked kale and avoid raw. The reason? It is a cruciferous vegetable. Cruciferous vegetables are fine for consumption if you have thyroid disease; just cook first.

7. Leaf Lettuce: Very similar to iceberg only leafy-er (is that a word?) More tender than iceberg perhaps but still firm enough to use as a "bun" for a chicken sandwich or a hamburger. A very mild taste; though not as sweet as iceberg. Cost is about the same as iceberg so try this the next time you are at the store. There are two varieties: red and green. Both are a beautiful leafy green! The green has a slight increase in nutrients over the red variety. This leafy green variety looks beautiful on a sandwich.

8. Radicchio: Another variety that is great for sitting out with dip. A beautiful food. Taste is bitter/peppery. Great choice if you are creating a mixed greens salad. Firm crisp leaves. Great in slaws. You can enjoy this cooked or raw.

9. Romaine: A popular lettuce. Crisp, bright, mildly sweet taste. Great for lettuce cups and to serve with a dip. Great to use as a

base when making homemade salad dressings, Caesar Salads are made with Romaine lettuce. Romaine hearts are also pretty good on the grill.

10. Spinach: A tender, dark leaf. We are all familiar with how versatile this vegetable is. I prefer fresh spinach from the produce department and chopped kale when buying frozen. Just a preference.

11. Watercress: Watercress has a strong peppery taste, similar to mustard greens. The leaves are tender, not crisp. Generally good with a sweet and sour profile and vinaigrettes which compliments the bitter leaves of the watercress, or used in combination with other types of lettuce.

This section is an excerpt from my book, Lettuce Amaze You! Are you looking for recipes and ideas to incorporate more healthy greens in your diet? Try my Lettuce Amaze You! Cookbook about lettuce: https://amzn.to/2umTrgf or go to Amazon and search isbn: 1540874931 or the title: Lettuce Amaze You by Paula C. Henderson

MUSHROOMS

- **Cremini Mushroom** is actually a baby Portobella.

- **Portobella** or Portabello: A rich meaty mushroom with a near bacon taste when sliced and fried.

- **White Button Mushroom**: the most common mushroom with a mild taste.

- **Shiitake** mushrooms are used in many Asian dishes and are said to have an anti-inflammatory effect on the body.

- **Porcino** Mushroom is a wild mushroom with a woodsy flavor.

VINEGAR

- Apple Cider Vinegar: Abbreviated as ACV, and should be in every kitchen for its versatility of use. Make a salad dressing or brighten up some cooked greens and otherwise heavy sauces.

- Balsamic Vinegar: Balsamic vinegar is made from fermented alcohol. Has a distinct sharp taste.

- Champagne Vinegar: A lighter taste and best used in cold dishes, not hot.

- Red Wine Vinegar: Best use in vinaigrettes and homemade dressings.

- Rice Vinegar: A nice mild flavor. Rice vinegar has a sweeter, less acidic flavor. Can be used in hot and cold dishes.

- Malt Vinegar: If you are gluten free you will want to avoid Malt Vinegar as it is made from barley. Traditionally known use is with fish and chips.

- White Wine: An excellent choice when you don't want to change the color of the produce itself. How to choose a vinegar much comes down to the same way we choose a wine. Use dark vinegars for heavier dark meats and vegetables and use a clear or "white" vinegar for lighter fare when paring with chicken and fish.

ARE YOU NUTRIENT SAVVY?

An excerpt from my book,
"Are You Nutrient Savvy?"
ISBN 1984004719

What's the difference between a vitamin, a mineral, and a nutrient?

Nutrients:

There are six (6) essential nutrients for the human body:

1. Proteins *see chapter 24*
2. Carbohydrates *see chapter 7*
3. Fats *see chapter 79*
4. Vitamins
5. Minerals
6. Water *see chapter 38*

Vitamins and minerals differ in basic ways.

Vitamins are organic and can be broken down by heat, air, or acid. **Vitamins** required by our body to function are:

- Vitamins A
- B1
- B2
- B3
- B6
- B12
- Vitamin C
- Vitamin D
- Vitamin E
- Vitamin K
- Folic Acid (vitamin B9)
- Pantothenic acid (vitamin B5)
- Biotin (vitamin B7).

Minerals are inorganic and hold on to their chemical structure. That means the **minerals** in soil and water easily find their way into your body through the plants, fish, animals, and fluids you consume.

Like vitamins, minerals are substances found in food that your body needs for growth and health. There are two kinds of minerals: macro minerals and trace minerals. Macro minerals are minerals your body needs in larger amounts. They include calcium, phosphorus, magnesium, sodium, potassium, and chloride.

Examples of minerals that are necessary for proper health include:

- Calcium
- iodine
- magnesium
- phosphorous
- potassium
- selenium
- sodium

- zinc

Each mineral plays a different role in maintaining proper health.

Abbreviations:

AI...............Adequate Intake
DRIs.............Dietary Reference Intakes
DV..............Daily Value
MCG...........micrograms (mcg), sometimes written as ug
MG.............milligrams (mg)
RDA............Recommended Daily Allowance

[There are 1,000 micrograms (**mcg**) in 1 milligram (mg)

(**RDA**) Recommended Dietary Allowance. The
amount of each vitamin and mineral needed
daily to meet the needs of nearly all healthy
people, as determined by the Food and Nutrition
Board of the Institute of Medicine.

Adequate Intake (**AI**). An AI is a recommended
intake level of certain nutrients based on estimates
of how much healthy people need. It's
used when there isn't enough data to establish
an RDA.

Percent Daily Value. What percentage of the **DV** (daily value)
in one serving of a food or supplement supplies.

For instance, if the label on a multivitamin (or food product)shows that 30
percent of the DV is provided, you'll need 70 percent from
other sources throughout the day to meet the recommended daily goal.

Your Daily Consumption

The healthiest foods you can consume are low carb vegetables.
They should make up approximately 70% of your daily food intake.
Vegetables have the widest variety of balanced nutrients for the body and many of them are good sources of Protein, Vitamin C, Calcium, and healthy carbs.

Healthy Proteins like meat, fish, and eggs, which are low to no carbs, should make up about 15% of your diet.
Remember that many vegetables offer good sources of protein.

Try for 10% Fat to be included with your diet.
Easily attained when using oils to cook with and when making salad dressings, sauces and general preparation of foods, not to mention good fats like Avocado and nuts. Just remember that nuts are generally high in carbohydrates so eat in limited portions.

Limit high carbohydrates to about 5% of your diet
and limit that to good healthy choices like a sweet potato, nuts, raw honey, and fruits.

*Do these things and I believe
you will fall at whatever
your naturally healthy
weight is for you!*

EXTRA BONUS: BASIC KNOWLEDGE

- We hear savory or sweet a lot lately. Savory means a dish that is not sweet; not a dessert. Sweet means sweet and generally refers to a dessert. A steak or stir fried vegetables are savory dishes. Pudding and ice cream are sweet dishes.

- To shock would be to immediately put food on ice upon taking out of boiling water. Usually after blanching. The intention is to stop the cooking process immediately.

- Boiling is vigorous big bubbles but simmering is subtle tiny bubbles. Sometimes referred to as a full boil.

- If you are making aioli or homemade mayo it is important that all your ingredients are room temperature and you are using a clean glass bowl that has been wiped with white distilled vinegar.

- To ensure your meat browns nicely make sure your meat has been patted dry and is room temperature before putting on the grill or in the skillet.

- Mold on cottage cheese or cream cheese means the food has gone bad. If mold is on a hard cheese you can just remove the mold and the remaining cheese if fine for consumption.

- How to keep your pasta from sticking: Give it plenty of room. Don't crowd the pasta when boiling. A large pot and plenty of water. Salt the water. Don't rinse the pasta if you will be serving it hot. If you are serving cold pasta shock it immediately in ice water and drain quickly. Always serve pasta dressed in the sauce by tossing it to coat each piece of pasta.

- The perfect technique to boil eggs: place eggs in saucepan. Cover completely with cold water. Place on the stove on high heat uncovered. As soon as the water comes to a full boil remove from heat, cover and set

your timer for 11 minutes.

According to
www.health.state.mn.us/foodsafety/cook/cooktemp.html

...the following are some safe cooking temperature tips:

Eggs and all ground meats must be cooked to **160°F**;

poultry and fowl to **165°F**;

and fresh meat steaks, chops and roasts to **145°F**

Get yourself a kitchen thermometer and stay safe in the kitchen.

About The Author:

Check out my cookbooks, journals and other books. Just go to
http://www.amazon.com/author/paulachenderson

If you have a moment I would really appreciate your leaving a review for this little booklet. Thank you so much!

Paula C. Henderson

Printed in Great Britain
by Amazon